ENGLISH
Alive

Level 1

Barry Scholes and Gill Atha

Collins Educational
An imprint of HarperCollinsPublishers

ENGLISH Alive

Level 1

Barry Scholes and Gill Atha

Contents

Collins Educational

a b c d e f g h i
j k l m n o p q
r s t u v w x
y z

Dan the Handyman

Look at the alphabet which Dan the Handyman has put up.

1   How many letters are there in the alphabet?

2   Can you say the alphabet without looking at the picture?
Ask a friend to test you.
If you get stuck try learning the first half from **a** to **m.**

3   Write these letters in the order they come in the alphabet.
b a c   y z x   v n d   w h p   s k f   g u m

4   The words in a dictionary are in alphabetical order.
b oy comes before **g** irl, because its first letter **b** comes before **g** in the alphabet. Write these words in alphabetical order.
cat, mouse, dog   orange, lemon, apple   roof, door, window
tree, flower, grass   yellow, blue, red   summer, winter, autumn

5   Look at the picture again. Besides Dan and the poster what other things can you see? Make a list of them in alphabetical order.

6   Some of the letters on Dan's poster are in red. We call these letters **vowels.** All the other letters are called **consonants.**
Write down the five vowels in alphabetical order.
Write down the twenty-one consonants in alphabetical order.

sentences

A sentence begins with a capital letter and ends with a full stop.

CAPITAL LETTERS

FULL STOPS

Write out these sentences beginning each one with a capital letter and ending with a full stop.

1   my uncle Tom is a very funny man
2   his jokes always make me laugh
3   he tried to be a magician at my birthday party
4   every trick went wrong
5   we all laughed until we cried

Myself
Katy Robinson wrote these sentences about herself.

My name is Katy Robinson.
I live at 31 Greentree Avenue.
I have a brother called Jason.
I go to Hilltop School.
My teacher is Miss Jones.
My favourite lesson is English.
When I grow up I would like to be a teacher.

Write seven sentences like Katy's, but change them so that they tell about you.
Remember the capital letters and full stops.
When you have finished draw a picture of yourself.

'When I was a lad Billy,' he said, 'which seems a long time ago mind, sometimes I couldn't get to sleep.'

'What did you used to do Grandad?' asked Billy, becoming interested.

'All sorts of things. First of all I used to get a great big book, with lots of interesting pictures in and look at that.'

'I've already done that,' said Billy. 'But it didn't make me feel tired like it usually does.'

'Well then, Billy, there was something that I never got to the end of. I used to try to think of an animal for each letter of the alphabet. Like a for antelope, b for bear, c for cat . . . you know. I never got to z for zebra — I was always asleep!'

'Mmmm,' Billy said, 'that's not a bad idea. Thanks Grandad, I'll try that.'

(From *Wide Awake Billy* by Marian Dillon)

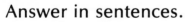

Answer in sentences.
1   Who is Billy talking to?
2   What was the first thing Grandad tried to get himself to sleep?
3   How did this work for Billy?
4   What was Grandad's second idea?
5   What do you do when you can't get to sleep? Write a few sentences about it.

Naming words

Naming words are the names of people and things.

zebra

book

pictures

1·2a   1·2b

1   Find these words in the story. Make a list of any other naming words you can find there. Draw a picture for each one.
2   Draw these word webs. Put in the names of seven things you find in each place.

classroom

street

kitchen

3   Choose one naming word from each word web. Write a sentence about it. Remember to begin with a capital letter and end with a full stop.
4   Choose three objects on your desk. Write their names in alphabetical order.
5   Choose five other objects in your classroom. Write their names in alphabetical order.

Writing

Complete these sentences in an interesting way. Remember to end each one with a full stop.

1   The boat sailed _____
2   I looked through the window and saw _____
3   It rained so hard _____
4   Last night I dreamed _____
5   Peter ran out of school _____
6   Sarah had to _____

7

UNIT 3 Magic carpet

The Sale went on for a week, and at the end there wasn't much left in the shop. Even the snuff had gone. We all went in to clear up on the Saturday, Charlie too.

Mr Markin said: 'You lads, see if there's anything left in the stock cupboard at the back,' so we went to have a look. There wasn't much. A few old cardboard boxes, a wellington boot, some paper bags, some empty ginger beer bottles, nothing very thrilling. Then Charlie said: 'What's this, Sam?' and pulled out a tatty old rug, thick with grease and dirt, and all rolled up in a bundle. We spread it out on the floor.

'It's a magic carpet,' said Charlie.

'Don't be daft,' I said. 'Magic carpets are bigger and cleaner and anyway, they're just made up.' (From *The Rug That Grew* by Adèle Geras)

Read the story carefully, and then read these sentences.
Are they true, false or doesn't the story tell you?
Write **True, False** or **Does not say** for your answers.

1   The sale lasted a week.
2   The snuff was still there.
3   The stock cupboard was brown.
4   The cupboard was empty.
5   Sam found the ring.
6   The rug was old.
7   Sam thought it was a magic carpet.
8   The shop belonged to Mr Markin.

To talk about

1   Do you think the rug really is a magic carpet? Why?
2   What do you think a magic carpet would be able to do?
3   In what other ways might a carpet be magic?

Special naming words

The special names of people, places and days always begin with a capital letter, like this: **Charlie   Sam   Saturday   Mr Markin   Smith Street**

1   Write your name and address. Make sure all the special names begin with a capital letter.
2   Write a friend's name and address.

Miss Green's Class

These children are all in Miss Green's class. Copy out her register. Begin each special naming word with a capital letter.

john	fields	26	marsden street
tracey	bates	13	clark road
sita	ahmed	12	grosvenor way
ruth	chalmers	123	clark road
martin	seddon	58	main avenue
gavin	jones	52	pinfold lane
david	giles	44	highfield close

Look at the first names of all the children in Miss Green's class. Now write the class in alphabetical order. The first two have been done for you.

David,   Gavin, _____

Question sentences

Some sentences ask questions:
   What's this, Sam?
Every question ends with a question mark.

Copy out these sentences.
Remember to put in a question mark.

What is your name
Where do you live
How old are you
When is your birthday
Who is your best friend

Now answer each question **in a complete sentence.** Remember to use a capital letter for each special name.

Writing

Write a story about a magic carpet. Begin your story like this:
   One day I found a magic carpet................

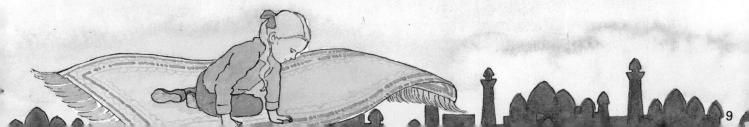

UNIT 4 Autumn on the farm

David woke up early.

The house was still quiet, but outside he could hear the usual early morning noises of the farm. There was the clank of buckets from the cow-shed, the busy clucking of the hens and from across the fields came the bellow of a bull.

David smiled to himself in a pleased sort of way. Quick as a flash, he was out of bed and dressing in warm clothes. The air was quite cold still, although it looked like being a fine Autumn day.

David was going to give his family a surprise. He had discovered a field where mushrooms grew — lots of them — little white buttons popping up overnight. If you got there early enough, you could pick as many as you liked.

(From *David and his Grandfather* by Pamela Rogers)

Copy these sentences about the story. Choose the correct word from the ones in brackets.

1 The house was _____. (noisy/peaceful)
2 David could _____ the hens on the farm. (see/hear)
3 He was _____. (happy/sad)
4 He put on his _____ clothes. (warm/wet)
5 David was going to give his family a _____. (treat/shock)
6 He had _____ a field of mushrooms. (planted/found)

To talk about

1 Talk about the busy day of a farmer. Draw pictures to show the different jobs he does, and write a sentence or two for each one.
2 Talk about the different foods grown and produced on our farms. List them under these headings: Fruit, Vegetables, Cereals, Dairy Products and Meat.

Animal Voices

Oh, dear! These animals do seem a little mixed up, don't they? Copy out these sentences giving each animal his own sound.

1   A cockerel shouts _____ to wake us up in the morning.
2   A pig says _____ and grunts his way through his breakfast.
3   The chickens _____ when they are laying their eggs.
4   The horse goes _____ as he gallops round his field.
5   The cow makes a _____ sound when it is time for milking.

Now write similar sentences about these animals and their sounds.

duck	lamb	turkey	donkey	bull
owl	dog	cat	frog	bird

Families
Copy this list of animal families into your book and fill in the blanks.

Father	Mother	Baby
_____	cow	calf
cock	hen	_____
_____	goose	gosling
boar	sow	_____
drake	_____	duckling
stallion	mare	_____
ram	ewe	_____

Writing
Make up a story about some farmyard animals whose voices get changed. Think up your own title. When you have finished your story, draw a picture of the animals.

UNIT 5 Bedtime Stories

Bedtime Stories

'Tell me a story,'
Says Witch's child.
About the Beast
So fierce and wild.

About a Ghost
That shrieks and groans.
A skeleton
That rattles bones.

About a Monster
Crawly-creepy
Something nice
To make me sleepy.
Lilian Moore

Answer in sentences.
1 Who wants to hear the story?
2 Why does the child want to hear the story?
3 What kind of story would the child like?
4 Who do you think the child is talking to in the poem?
5 Would you choose such a frightening story at bedtime? Why?

Describing words

Look again at the poem. Can you find what it says about the Beast?
  It says he is **fierce** and **wild.**
These two words tell us what the Beast is like. They are **describing words.**

Draw these word webs in your book. Add as many describing words as you can for each one.

ghost   rabbit   school   myself   witch

Question sentences

Write down the six sentences that ask questions.

1 What is that
2 Tell me a story
3 Is the witch reading the story
4 Do you like stories about witches
5 I like chocolate cake
6 Where is he going
7 She opened the book
8 Who is afraid of ghosts
9 I am going to school
10 How many sweets did you eat

DON'T FORGET THE QUESTION MARK.

Complete these question sentences in your own way.

1 What is . . . .   5 When did it . . . .
2 Do we . . . .   6 Did you . . . .
3 Who went . . . .   7 How many times . . . .
4 Where can he . . . .   8 Why can't . . . .

Writing

Write a bedtime story for the witch's child.
Make it as frightening and exciting as you can.

13

UNIT 6 A WARM CAVE

'I've got it! I've got it at last!'

Grump's eyes sparkled with excitement as he crouched in the centre of his cave. They reflected the light of something that danced and flickered before him. It was a gaily burning fire. Grump had never been so pleased with himself.

'Said I couldn't do it, didn't they? Laughed at me, they did.'

Grump hadn't lit the fire himself. At that time no caveman could make fire. But it had been a dry summer. Lightning had struck a tree in the forest, and set it alight. Only Grump of all the cavemen had thought of taking a smouldering stick from the fire. The others had mocked him, but now he had a small fire of his very own.

'And it's lovely, simply lovely!' he chortled. 'Won't they be jealous when the cold weather comes.'

The catch was that the weather was still warm and Grump's cave was so full of smoke that he could hardly breathe. At last he could stand it no more.

'I'll just pop outside for some fresh air. Need more wood for my marvellous fire, anyway.'

(From *Grump and the Hairy Mammoth* by Derek Sampson)

Answer these questions about the story.

1 Where was Grump?
2 Why was he so pleased?
3 How had he got the fire?
4 What made Grump leave his cave?
5 What was Grump going to collect?
6 Imagine that you are Grump.
  Where would you go to collect firewood?
  Write what happens to you whilst you are collecting it.

14

Homes

In the story, Grump lives in a cave. Today we live in houses, but there are many different kinds. Find out who lives in each house and then write a sentence about it, like this:

Janet lives in a bungalow.

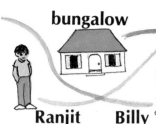
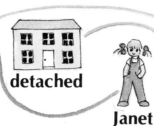

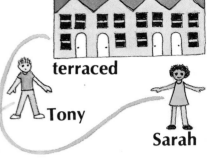

bungalow

detached

semi-detached

terraced

Ranjit   Billy

Janet

Tony

Sarah

One and More Than One

We say one stick, but two stick**s**.
We say one bush, but two bush**es**.

Copy and finish these sentences in the same way.

1   We say one boat, but two _____.
2   We say one fox, but four _____.
3   We say one day, but seven _____.
4   We say one potato, but two _____.
5   We say one rabbit, but many _____.

Sentences

Grump has written about his fire. Because he has never been to school his sentences are not very good. He has missed out all his capital letters, full stops and question marks, and some of his sentences do not even make sense.
   Write Grump's sentences properly.

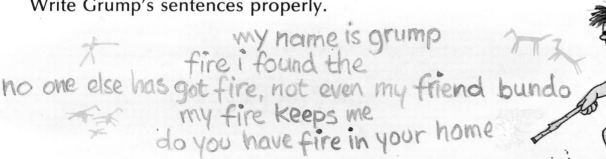

my name is grump
fire i found the
no one else has got fire, not even my friend bundo
my fire keeps me
do you have fire in your home

To talk about

1   Would you like to live in a cave? What do you think it would be like?
   What sort of things would you miss?

2   Make a list of different homes from all over the world.
   What would it be like to live in them?

3   If you could change your home for a completely different one, what would you choose and why?

UNIT 7 — *I Mustn't Forget*

Do you ever forget something you've been told? Bobby Brewster does and so do his mother and father. Bobby forgets because he doesn't always listen properly to instructions in the first place and they go in one ear and out of the other. Mr and Mrs Brewster forget because the older they get, the more difficult it is to remember.

There are all sorts of ways, of course, to help you to remember things. Bobby Brewster sometimes ties a knot in his handkerchief. That idea works, but it annoys his mother because the knots get very tight to untie and they make his handkerchiefs grubby. Still, it is better than biting holes in his handkerchiefs, which is another habit of his.

(From *Bobby Brewster's Wishbone* by H. E. Todd)

Answer these questions about the story.

1 Why does Bobby forget things?
2 Why do Mr and Mrs Brewster forget things?
3 What does Bobby do to try to make himself remember?
4 Why does this annoy his mother?
5 What do you do when you want to remember something?

Remembering

Some people tie knots in their handkerchiefs when they want to remember something, other people find it easier to write things down.

Bobby wrote these instructions for making a cup of tea, but they are in the wrong order. Put the instructions in the right order for him.

Pour the tea in the cup.
Put water in the kettle.
Add milk and sugar and then it is ready to drink.
Put the kettle on.
Put tea in the teapot.
When the water has boiled pour it in the teapot.

A and An

We say **a** ball but **an** owl.

If the naming word begins with a vowel, **a e i o u**, then we must use **an** and not **a**.

Put **a** or **an** in front of these words.

mouse	elephant	igloo	giraffe	hat	policeman
school	orange	apple	egg	umbrella	balloon

Sentences

We can join two short sentences together by using the word **and.**
Bobby went to the bus stop. Bobby waited for the bus.
Bobby went to the bus stop **and** waited for the bus.

Join these sentences together using **and.**
1   Mum went to the shop. She bought some potatoes.
2   I went to Janet's house. We played with her dolls.
3   I opened the window. I looked outside.
4   Humpty Dumpty fell off the wall. He hurt his head.
5   My brother likes sweets. He likes chocolate.

Writing

Have you ever forgotten something really important? What happened? How did you feel?
Write a story about forgetting something important. Don't forget to say how you finally remembered it.

Words which might help you:

think	remember	memory
forget	forgetful	important

The Clown

I like to see
The spotted clown
Throwing dishes
In the air.
When they've started
Coming down
He looks as though
He didn't care,
But catches each one
Perfectly,
Over and over,
Every time,
One and two and
One-two-three-
Like a pattern
Or a rhyme.
Dorothy Aldis

Copy and complete.

1   The title of the poem is 'The _____'   (clown/juggler)
2   The clown is wearing _____ clothes.   (stripey/spotty)
3   He is _____.   (juggling/playing)
4   The clown is throwing _____ in the air.   (balls/plates)
5   When the plates come down the clown _____ them.   (drops/catches)

To talk about

Talk about a clown you have seen in real life or on television. How did the clown make you laugh? Draw a picture of him.

Describing words

Complete this word web by adding words which could describe a clown.

clumsy   amusing

clown   fat

18

Here are some more describing words:

| clever | long | funny | fierce | beautiful |

Copy and complete these sentences by choosing the best describing word.

1 The _____ lion is jumping through a hoop.
2 I can see a _____ lady riding a horse.
3 Look at the _____ clown.
4 The dancing horse is very _____.
5 The lion tamer has a _____ whip.

Now put these describing words into sentences of your own.

| happy | red | young | fat |

Opposites

The opposite of **high** is **low**.
The opposite of **wet** is **dry**.

Answer these questions in sentences.
The first one has been done for you.

1 What is the opposite of **day**?
   The opposite of day is night.
2 What is the opposite of **up**?
3 What is the opposite of **out**?
4 What is the opposite of **heavy**?
5 What is the opposite of **rich**?
6 What is the opposite of **tall**?

Writing

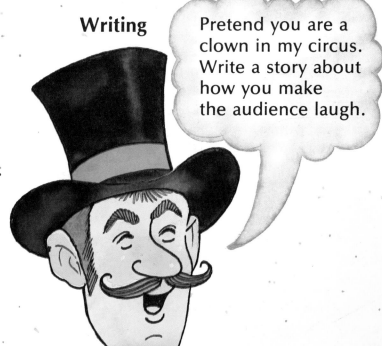

Pretend you are a clown in my circus. Write a story about how you make the audience laugh.

UNIT 9 👀 A monster in the cupboard 👀

'You haven't been scared of the cupboard since you were Dawn's age,' said Mum. 'Don't be so silly. You went in the cupboard only yesterday. Now go and get the dustpan and brush this minute.'

Holly went to the cupboard under the stairs and peeped round the door. It looked very dark inside. But Holly wasn't a baby. She was big. She decided to be brave. She stepped over the vacuum cleaner and she ignored the pruning shears hanging on the hook. She found the dustpan and brush straight away.

She smiled in the dark. She wondered how she could ever have been silly enough to believe in the monster. And then she heard a rustle. Something was moving at the back of the cupboard.

(From *The Monster in the Cupboard* by Jacqueline Wilson)

Read the story. Write **True, False** or **Does not say** for each of these sentences.

1 Holly had never been in the cupboard before.
2 Holly was eight years old.
3 It was dark inside the cupboard.
4 She fell over a vacuum cleaner.
5 There was a wooden box inside the cupboard.
6 She heard a rustling sound.
7 She could not find the dustpan and brush.

To talk about

1 What do you think was in the cupboard?
2 What do you think will happen next?

20

Action words

Holly peeps. **Holly** is a naming word. **Peeps** is an action word. It tells us what Holly does.

Choose the action word that goes with each of these naming words.

1	Dogs	6	Fire	sing	ring
2	Doors	7	Bells	hum	gallop
3	Birds	8	Fish	roar	bark
4	Lions	9	Bees	slam	swim
5	Rain	10	Horses	pours	burns

1·9b

Add action words to these word webs.

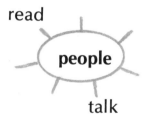

read

people

talk

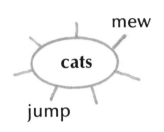

mew

cats

jump

1·9c

Joining sentences

Sometimes we use **but** to join two sentences.

Holly is big. Dawn is small.
Holly is big, **but** Dawn is small.

We use **but** because **big** is the opposite of **small.**

Join these sentences with **but.**

1 The sun is bright.   It is dark in the cupboard.
2 It was a hot day.   The sea was cold.
3 My hands are clean.   Your hands are dirty.
4 John is happy.   His friend is sad.
5 Giants are tall.   Dwarfs are small.
6 Jill comes to school early.   Debby comes late.
7 I turn left when I leave school.   You turn right.
8 The red door is open.   The blue door is shut.

Writing

Some children say that a monster lives in your school, and comes out at night. Write a story about it.

21

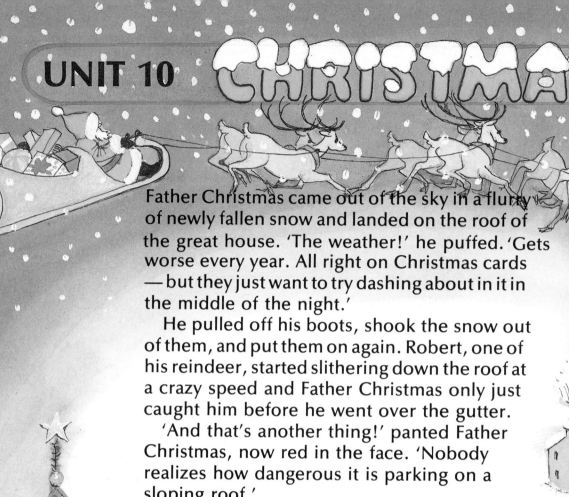

UNIT 10 CHRISTMAS

Father Christmas came out of the sky in a flurry of newly fallen snow and landed on the roof of the great house. 'The weather!' he puffed. 'Gets worse every year. All right on Christmas cards — but they just want to try dashing about in it in the middle of the night.'

He pulled off his boots, shook the snow out of them, and put them on again. Robert, one of his reindeer, started slithering down the roof at a crazy speed and Father Christmas only just caught him before he went over the gutter.

'And that's another thing!' panted Father Christmas, now red in the face. 'Nobody realizes how dangerous it is parking on a sloping roof.'

He roped his six reindeer together and tied them to the chimney stack.

(From *Princess Polly to the Rescue* by Mary Lister)

Answer these questions about the story.

1 Name two things which Father Christmas grumbled about.
2 Why did he pull off his boots?
3 What happened to Robert?
4 How did Father Christmas stop his reindeer from falling off the roof?
5 What do you think he will do next?

To talk about

1 Are you surprised that Father Christmas grumbles about delivering presents? Why? Which part of his job do you think he likes best?
2 Imagine you are Father Christmas. Tell the story of your hard work on Christmas Eve.

Writing

Write a letter to Father Christmas saying what you would like him to bring you. Say why you would like these presents.

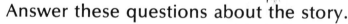

Christmas crackers

Sort out the jumbled letters to find out what was in the crackers.

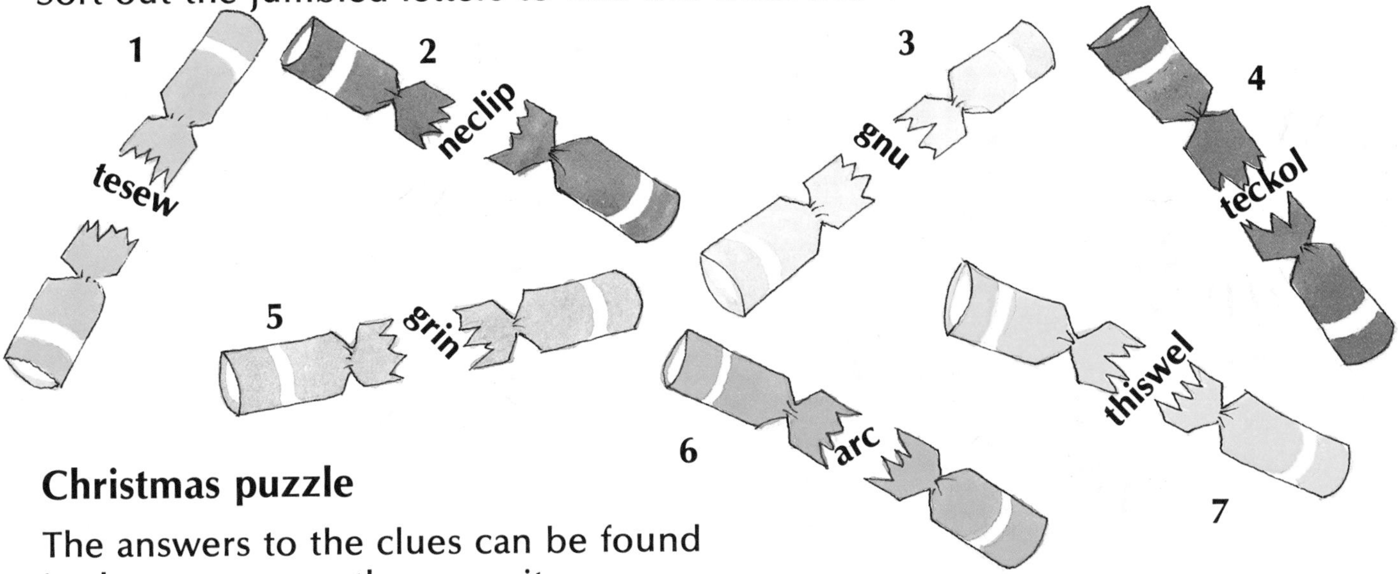

1 tesew

2 neclip

3 gnu

4 teckol

5 grin

6 arc

7 thiswel

Christmas puzzle

The answers to the clues can be found in the passage on the opposite page.

1 It gets worse every year.
2 They were full of snow.
3 He nearly fell off the roof.
4 Father Christmas came out of the ____ .
5 How many reindeer?
6 He tied his reindeer to it.
7 Robert is one of these.
8 Where he parked.

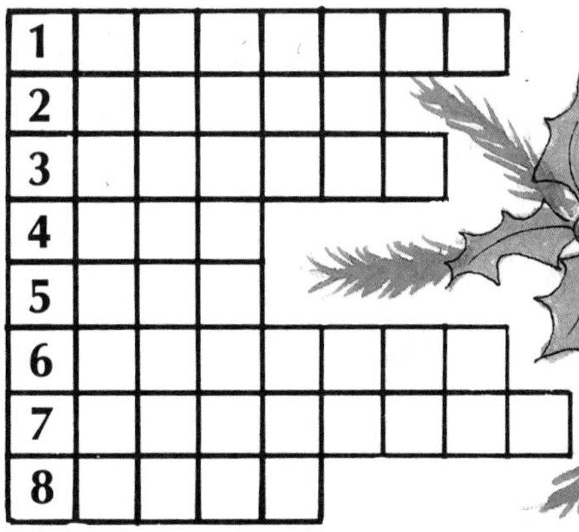

Join these sentences using **and** or **but**.

1 Adam wanted a computer for Christmas.   Santa brought him a bicycle.
2 Father Christmas delivered all his presents.   He was home for breakfast.
3 Robert the reindeer nearly slipped off the roof.   Santa saved him.
4 I found the crossword easy.   David found it difficult.
5 Mary wrote a letter.   She posted it to Father Christmas.
6 I went to a party at school.   I won a prize.

How many words can you make from the letters of **Christmas?**

1·10a
1·10b
1·10c

23

Mr Fisher spun round to face the class and said in a Wake Up At The Back voice, 'A Red Letter Day! Who can tell me what that is?'

Clare Wilkins's hand shot up, but the rest of the class were too sleepy to give their usual groan at her eagerness.

'Sir! I know Sir!' she announced proudly. 'It's an important day. A special day.' Mr Fisher beamed at her.

'Quite right, Clare.' He looked round the rest of the class without much hope. 'I don't suppose anyone knows *why* special days are called Red Letter Days?' There was a heavy silence, except for what might have been a faint snore from Banger Morgan. His head was very low over his desk. Even Clare did not answer.

The head sighed and explained about saints' days and holidays being marked in red on old-fashioned calendars.

(From *Red Letter Day* by Alexa Romanes)

1 What do you think a 'Wake Up At The Back' voice is?
2 What do the rest of the class usually do when Clare Wilkins answers?
3 Why did they not do so on this occasion?
4 What is a red letter day?
5 Why is it so called?

To talk about

1 Make a list of red letter days.
2 Some days are special only to you and your family. Which are your red letter days? Why?
3 How are red letter days celebrated?

Writing

Find a partner in the class. Each of you write a letter inviting the other to a party. Remember to say where the party is and when it begins.

Exchange letters and write a reply to your friend's invitation.

Months of the year

Notice that the name of each month begins with a capital letter.
That is because they are all special names.
Copy and complete these sentences with the name of a month.

1 New Year's Day is in _____.
2 Christmas Day is in _____.
3 My birthday is in _____.
4 March comes after _____.
5 September comes before _____.
6 _____ comes before January.

JANUARY
FEBRUARY
MARCH
APRIL
MAY
JUNE
JULY
AUGUST
SEPTEMBER
OCTOBER
NOVEMBER
DECEMBER

The calendar

Here is a page from a calendar. Look at it carefully and find the answers to the questions below.

DECEMBER

Sun	Mon	Tue	Wed	Thur	Fri	Sat
.	1	2	3	4	5	6
7	8	9	10	11	12	13
14	15	16	17	18	19	20
21	22	23	24	25	26	27
28	29	30	31	.	.	.

1 For which month is this a calendar page?
2 Which day is the first of the month?
3 Which day is the last of the month?
4 How many days are there on this calendar page?
5 How many Sundays are there in this month?
6 How many Mondays are there in this month?
7 What is special about the two red letter days?

Learn this rhyme

Thirty days hath September,
April, June and November;
All the rest have thirty-one,
Excepting February alone,
And that has twenty-eight days clear
And twenty-nine in each leap year.

Spooky Towers

In the dark and stormy hours,
A stranger came to Spooky Towers.
A servant showed him to a room,
Full of cobwebs, dust and gloom.

And as the stranger fell asleep,
Around him things began to creep:
Skeletons with jangling chains,
Monsters' heads with dead men's brains.

Spooks and spectres round his bed,
Cold dead fingers touched his head;
And waking screaming in the night,
The wretched stranger died of fright.

Now in the dark and stormy hours,
A new ghost screams at Spooky Towers.

Barry Scholes

1   When did the stranger arrive at Spooky Towers?
2   How do we know his room was not clean?
3   What sound could be heard as he fell asleep?
4   What was it that made him wake up screaming?
5   Who is the new ghost at Spooky Towers?

Rhyming Words

Bed has the same sound as **head.** The two words rhyme.
Write down four other pairs of words from the poem which rhyme.

Making Rhymes

To find words which rhyme with **bad** we can try adding different letters to **-ad.**

d   + ad   =   dad
h   + ad   =   had
m   + ad   =   mad
p   + ad   =   pad
s   + ad   =   sad

Find as many words as you can to rhyme with each of the following.

1 bat **2** pot **3** day **4** meet **5** rain **6** hill

Which words have the same sound as the word in capital letters?

1 CREEP leap green creek asleep
2 COLD bolt fold could told
3 CHAIN train same lane fame
4 STORM torn warm rain form
5 DARK mark dim lark part
6 ROOM soon broom noon loom
7 SCREAM lean mean cream team
8 DUST must dish mist rust

Sounds

1 The sound of jangling chains can be heard at Spooky Towers.
Write down five other sounds you might hear in a haunted house.

2 A door **slams.** Rain **patters.** Write a sentence to show what sounds these make.
   a A clock . . . .   **b** A bell . . . .   **c** A whip . . . .
   d Steam . . . .   **e** A cork . . . .   **f** Leaves . . . .

3 What makes these sounds?
   a bang **b** drip **c** chime **d** hoot **e** crinkle **f** twang

Spelling

Some ghosts make no sound at all. The letters in some words are like these ghosts. When we say the words we cannot hear them, but when we write them the silent letters appear.

Write these words and underline the silent letters.

1 know **2** climb **3** could **4** knock **5** dumb **6** comb
7 write **8** would **9** hymn **10** knee

Writing

Imagine you visit Spooky Towers on a dark and stormy night. Write about the sounds you hear and the frightening things that happen to you.

The puppy

I came home from school, and there in the kitchen was a quivering lump of a little thing. A bundle of black and white hair with a stubby tail at one end and a shiny black nose at the other.

You've guessed. It wasn't a hippopotamus or an elephant. It wasn't a snake or a baby giraffe. (It wasn't even a kitten.) It was a dog. Dog. D-O-G spells what I have been trying to describe.

It must have been love at first sight, because as soon as I walked into the kitchen, he opened his eyes, waggled to his feet and trotted over towards me (I was so surprised I just stood there open-mouthed.) He looked up at me wagging his tail as if he had been waiting for me all his life. If I'd had a tail I would have wagged it as well. Instead, I picked him up and hugged him and ran into the living-room where we rolled around on the carpet and chased each other and played puppy games until Dad made me sit down for tea.

(From *The Stowaways* by Roger McGough)

1 How do you know the writer was surprised to see the puppy?
2 What did the puppy do when he saw the writer?
3 What games did they play together?
4 Why did they have to stop their play?
5 Describe the puppy.

To talk about

Describe your pet, or one you would like to have, but don't say what it is. Talk about the amusing things it does. See if the class can guess what it is from your description.

Writing

Imagine you are the writer of the story. Write an entry in your diary for the day you got your puppy.

Alphabetical order

| a b c d e f g h i j k l m n o p q r s t u v w x y z |

Look at these words: **pet   puppy.**
They both begin with the letter **p.**

To put them in alphabetical order we have to
look at the second letter: p **e** t   p **u** ppy.

The alphabetical order of these letters is **e   u.**
So the alphabetical order of the words is: p **e** t   p **u** ppy.

1.13b

Write these words in alphabetical order. Look closely at the second letters.

1	play	puppy	present	6	bird	boot	bun	blind
2	cat	catch	climb	7	moon	mat	meat	must
3	run	rip	ring	8	tune	tell	tall	throw
4	door	dance	drive	9	shoe	sun	slow	see
5	nest	name	nut	10	grass	give	glass	gun

Group names   Look at these pictures.

They are all dogs.

What are these?

1   They are all _____.

2   They are all _____.

3   They are all _____.

Rewrite each group in alphabetical order. Give each group a name.

1	donkey	cat	duck	horse	They are all _____.
2	peas	carrots	potatoes	beans	They are all _____.
3	plum	peach	lemon	strawberry	They are all _____.
4	pink	blue	brown	purple	They are all _____.
5	sock	shirt	skirt	scarf	They are all _____.

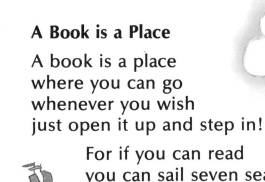

UNIT 14 Books

A Book is a Place

A book is a place
where you can go
whenever you wish
just open it up and step in!

    For if you can read
    you can sail seven seas
    explore lost kingdoms
    with magic keys . . .

      Climb snowy mountains,
      Fly to the moon,
      Speak with ghosts,
      Hear mermaids croon . . .

      Swim with whales
      through sea-green depths,
      Tame wild horses and . . .

        When you come back
        and close your book
        and sit there with a dreamy,
        faraway look . . .

        It's because you
        know you can go
        anywhere you want
        whenever you wish —
        just open a book and step in!   *Clyde Watson*

Write a list of **eight** things the poem says you can do in the pages of a book.
Tell the class about your favourite book and why you like it.

Writing

Choose **one** of the adventures in the poem and write your own story about it.
When you have written it exchange it with one written by a classmate. Check
each other's work. Then copy your story, with any corrections, into a class *Book
of Adventure* and draw pictures to illustrate your story.

Things to do

1 If you were given book tokens to buy any **five** books which would you
    choose. Why?

2 Paint a picture showing an exciting moment in your favourite story.

A Library

The books in a library are arranged into two groups.

Fiction (stories)
The Stowaways — Roger McGough
The BFG — Roald Dahl
The Sick Cow — H. E. Todd
Red Letter Day — Alexa Romanes
Freckle Juice — Judy Blume

Non-fiction (books of information)
Autumn on the Farm
My Class Goes to the Library
Looking After Pets

Fiction books are about imaginary people and adventures.
Non-fiction books are about real things and real people.

Write these titles under the headings **Fiction** and **Non-fiction.**

Flat Stanley
Let's Visit the West Indies
My Class Looks After Pets
Bobby Brewster's Wishbone
Tales from China
Magnetism and Electricity
Fantastic Mr. Fox

How to be a Detective
Princess Polly to the Rescue
Tales of a One-way Street
Life in Castle Times
A Village in Pakistan
Billy Boot's Brainwave
One Dragon's Dream

Finding a fiction book

To find a fiction book in a library we need to know who wrote it. This is because the first letter of the author's surname decides which shelf it goes on.
Freckle Juice by Judy Blume goes on shelf **B** because B is the first letter of her surname, **B**lume.
The BFG by Roald Dahl goes on shelf **D** because Dahl begins with D.

1 Write the names of these authors in the order their books would be found in a library.

Marion Dillon	Adele Geras	Pamela Rodgers	Derek Sampson
Althea	Jeff Brown	H. E. Todd	Mary Lister
Dorothy Edwards	Helen Cresswell	Janet McNeill	Pamela Oldfield

2 Write these names in the same way, but where surnames begin with the same letter, look closely at the second letter.

Leila Berg	Phyllis Arkle	Donald Bisset	Jill Murphy
M. S. Barry	Michael Bond	Joan Aiken	Margaret Mahy

You have now written two lists of authors whose books are very popular with children of your age. Look for their books the next time you visit a library. Just open a book and step in!

FACES

Andrew Marcus wanted freckles. Nicky Lane had freckles. He had about a million of them. They covered his face, his ears and the back of his neck. Andrew didn't have any freckles. He had two warts on his finger. But they didn't do him any good at all. If he had freckles like Nicky, his mother would never know if his neck was dirty. So he wouldn't have to wash. And then he'd never be late for school.

Andrew had plenty of time to look at Nicky's freckles. He sat right behind him in class. Once he even tried to count them. But when he got to eighty-six Miss Kelly called, 'Andrew . . . are you paying attention?'

'Yes, Miss Kelly,' Andrew said.

'Good, Andrew. I'm glad to hear that. Now will you please pick up your chair and join your reading group? We're all waiting for you.'

Andrew stood up in a hurry. His reading group giggled. Especially Sharon. He couldn't stand that Sharon. She thought she knew everything!

(From *Freckle Juice* by Judy Blume)

Read the passage. Write **True, False** or **Does not say** for each of these sentences.

1 Andrew had two warts on his finger.
2 Andrew had no freckles on his face.
3 Nicky had eighty-six freckles.
4 Sharon had freckles.
5 Andrew did not like Miss Kelly.
6 Andrew did not like washing his nec[k]
7 Nicky sat behind Andrew in class.

To talk about

1 Do you think Andrew was right in thinking that if he had freckles he would never have to wash his neck? Why do you think so?
2 Explain why Andrew thinks he would never be late for school if he had freckles.
3 The passage is from a book called *Freckle Juice*. What do you think such a juice might do? What might its ingredients be? What might happen if too much were used?

Writing   Invent your own magic medicine. Say what it is for, and write a recipe. Make a label for your medicine with a picture and instructions for use. Glue it on to a bottle. Write a story about it.

Describing words

1 Match each face with one of these describing words.

> happy   sad   frightened   beautiful   surprised

2 Draw a face to fit each of these describing words.

> old   young   ugly   bored   sleepy   angry

Identity parade

Fingers Flanagan

Snatcher Smith

Burglar Bill

Robin Bankes

Jemmy Johnson

> He had short ginger hair
> and a scar on his left cheek.
> Or was it his right cheek?
> I'm not sure about that.
> He had a moustache though,
> a long droopy one.

Mrs. Jones gave the police this description
of the man who robbed her. Who was the thief?

Dictionary work

Use your dictionary. Write each word and its meaning in your book.

> forehead   scalp   complexion   forearm

Which is the odd-man-out? Why?

Writing

Look carefully at your neighbour's face. Pay particular attention to colour and
length of hair, eye colour, ears, nose and mouth. Look for any special features
such as freckles. Now write a description for the class to recognise.

Picture 1.

Picture 2.

Is seeing believing?

1 Look at Picture 1. What impossible thing seems to be happening?
2 Why should the girl appear tired, but the boy not?
3 Do you think such steps could be built? Why?
4 Look at Picture 2. If you stare at the black squares, what do you see appearing in the white spaces between them?
5 What happens if you look at one of these grey dots?
6 Do you think seeing is believing? Why?

Pictogram to show the favourite colours of Class 1

● = boy   ● = girl

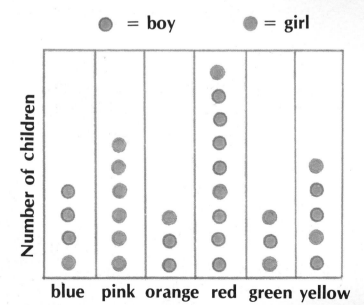

Number of children

blue pink orange red green yellow

1 Which is the most popular colour?
2 Which is the least popular colour?
3 How many children prefer orange?
4 How many children prefer yellow?
5 Which colour is liked only by the girls?
6 How many more boys than girls prefer red?
7 How many more girls than boys prefer green?
8 How many more boys than girls are there in Class 1?
9 Make a similar pictogram for the favourite colours of your class.

Everyday expressions

What do you think these everyday expressions mean?

with flying colours   in the pink

feeling blue   a white elephant

green with envy   to keep it dark

looking at things through rose-coloured spectacles

Make a class *Book of Everyday Expressions*. Write each expression with its meaning. Draw a picture for each one.

Is and Are

Gill **is** reading.   David **is** reading.   Gill and David **are** reading.

1·16a

1·16b

We use **is** when we are speaking of **one** person or thing.
We use **are** when we are speaking of **more than one** person or thing.

Put **is** or **are** in the spaces:
1   Matthew _____ watching television.
2   Your books _____ on your desk.
3   His favourite colour _____ red.
4   The first day of the week _____ Sunday.
5   June, July and August _____ summer months.
6   Calves _____ baby cows.

Was and Were

We use **was** when we are speaking of **one** person or thing, but we use **were** for **more than one**.

Put **was** or **were** in the spaces:

1   Helen _____ late for school.   4   The chocolates _____ good.
2   The weather _____ cold.   5   The window _____ broken.
3   The kittens _____ playful.   6   The men _____ laughing.

Writing

These magic spectacles once belonged to a wizard.
Suppose you found them and put them on. What might
you see? How would everyday things look?
Write a story about how you found the spectacles, and
the adventures you had when wearing them. Draw or
paint a picture to go with your story.

35

Sounds

The whistling of the wind,
The pattering of the rain,
The tapping of the hail-stones
Upon the window-pane.
  The splashing of your gum-boots
  In the puddles of the lane,
  The gurgling of the water
  As it rushes down the drain.
The cooing of the pigeon,
The crying of the eagle,
The snorting and the sniffing
And the barking of the beagle.
  The slam of a large door,
  The slam of a small,
  The crack of a rifle,
  The bounce of a ball
The very very quiet sounds —
The walking of some ants;
The very very noisy sounds —
The run of elephants. *Alexander Kennedy*

1 List all the sounds of weather mentioned in the poem. Begin like this: "the whistling of the wind, the pattering of . . ."
2 List all the sounds of animals and birds mentioned in the poem.
3 List three quiet sounds and three loud sounds from the poem.
4 Which of the sounds in the poem do you like best? Say why.
5 Which do you like least? Why?
6 Make two lists of sounds not mentioned in the poem under the headings **Pleasant sounds** and **Unpleasant sounds.** Read the poem again, and then write your own poem about your favourite sounds.

Sounds

Each verse of the poem is mainly about one kind of sound.
Read each verse and choose a word to complete these sentences.

 loud animals things weather water quiet
1 The first verse is mainly about the sounds of the _____ .
2 The second verse is about the sounds of _____ .
3 Verse three is about the sounds of birds and _____ .
4 The fourth verse is about the sounds made by _____ .
5 The last verse is about very _____ sounds and very _____ sounds.

The **ring** of a bell. The **hoot** of an owl.
What sounds are these?

1 The _____ of a drum.
2 The _____ of a frog.
3 The _____ of a mouse.
4 The _____ of steam.
5 The _____ of a seagull.
6 The _____ of a bee.

Telephone directory

Hall, A., 9 Linkwood Crescent	007-321 6295
Hall, Bernard, 121 Bowmore Avenue	007-467 2731
Hall, C.K., 1 Highland Park	007-463 7498
Hall, David, 7 Rosebank Street	007-321 4528
Hall, Glenn, 21 Grant Street	007-463 7233

Use the telephone directory to complete these sentences.
1 Bernard Hall's phone number is 007- _____ 2731.
2 C.K. Hall lives at _____ Highland Park.
3 Glenn Hall lives at 21 _____ Street.
4 A. Hall's phone number is 007-321 _____ .
5 _____ Hall lives at 7 Rosebank Street.

Hear and Here

Look at these sentences:
Come over **here.**   I can **hear** the rustle of leaves.

Put **hear** or **here** in these sentences.
1 I came _____ yesterday.
2 Listen carefully and you will _____ the babble of a stream.
3 Did you _____ the howl of a wolf?
4 I lost it somewhere round _____ .
5 Come _____ and you will _____ the dripping of water.

Sentence making

Look at these words: **radio   Karen   listened.**
We can use them to make a sentence: Karen listened to the radio.

Make sentences with these words. Remember the capital letters and full stops.
1 we   lion   ran   roared
2 Paul   holidays   going
3 men   hole   road   dug
4 deaf   man   knocked   down   bus
5 Lynn   shout   heard   someone
6 Jones   chased   broken window   boys

37

TOUCH

The Feel of Things

I like roughness in warm towels
Smoothness in cool sheets;
I like to feel the stinging rain
Needling on my cheeks.
I like to feel soft bedroom rugs
When my feet are bare,
I like the new-washed silkiness
Of our baby's hair.

A. Elliott-Cannon

1   What does the poet like about the feel of warm towels?
2   What kind of sheets does he like?
3   What does he like about rain? Do you agree with him? Why?
4   Which soft things does he like?
5   What does he like to touch with his feet?

To talk about

1   Which things do you like the feel of?   Which things do you not like?
2   Think of the times you have been told not to touch something.
    Why do you think this was?
    What sort of things might it be dangerous to touch?
3   What is texture?
4   What does it feel like if you have 'pins and needles'?
5   What does it mean to 'rub someone up the wrong way'?

Describing words

1   Here are some words which describe how things feel:

smooth	rough	sharp	hot	cold	wet
jagged	spongy	silky	soft	hard	prickly

How many more can you think of?

Set up a touch table in your classroom. Collect items which you can touch.
Feel them and think of words to describe them.

2   Give as many describing words as you can for each of these:
    a) velvet   **b)** ice   **c)** jelly   **d)** mud   **e)** sandpaper   **f)** polystyrene
    g) a pin   **h)** plasticine   **i)** glue

3   Make lists of objects under these headings:
    smooth,   rough,   soft,   sharp,   prickly.

The comma

Commas are needed to separate words in a list. Look at the commas in this sentence:

The stone was round, smooth, wet and cold.

Copy these sentences, putting in the commas.

1 The knife was long shiny and very sharp.
2 Pins needles nails and screws are all sharp.
3 On our touch table we had pebbles shells sandpaper silk and clay.
4 In his pocket he had marbles chocolate money and a toy car.

Writing

Go to your class touch table. Choose **ten** objects.
Write sentences for each one describing how it feels, and what it reminds you of.
This is what Anita wrote about two of her objects:

The pebble feels cool, smooth and heavy. It reminds me of holidays on the beach.
The hairbrush feels prickly. It reminds me of a hedgehog.

Now write about your objects.

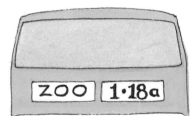

More than One

We say one pin, but two pin**s**.
The usual way to make a naming word **plural,** or **more than one,** is to add the letter **-s.**
We cannot do this with all words. When naming words end with the letters **-s, -ss, x, -z, -ch** or **-sh,** we add **-es** instead:

We say brush, brush**es**; touch, touch**es**; box, box**es**; witch, witch**es**.

Copy and complete.

1 one bus   three _____
2 a cardboard box   two old, wooden _____
3 an exciting match   many cricket _____
4 one kiss   several _____
5 a broken dish   six clean, shiny _____

Finding out

Find out who Louis Braille was, and why blind people all over the world are grateful to him.

39

The King's Cake

Once upon a time there was a very fat King who said to his very thin cook, 'Bake me a cake! The lightest, nicest, scrumpiest cake you've ever made.'

So the cook got a big bowl and two dozen eggs and some butter and five pounds of flour and a pound of yeast.

He mixed the flour and the eggs and the butter in the big bowl, then put in the yeast. Then he lit the gas and when the oven was hot he put the cake in.

Soon there was a lovely smell of baking cake, and the King came running in.

'My, my!' he said. 'What a lovely smell. I'm sure it's going to be a delicious cake, cook.'

(From *Time and again Stories* by Donald Bissett)

1   Is the thin cook a lady or a man? How do you know?
2   Did the cook use more flour than yeast?
3   Why do you think the cook uses yeast?
4   What makes the King think the cake will be delicious?
5   What do you think the cake might have tasted like?
6   Make a list of your favourite cooking smells.

Here are the cook's instructions for making the King's cake. But look, they are all muddled up! Write the instructions in the correct order.

Put the cake in the oven.
Weigh the flour, yeast and butter.
When it is cool it is ready to eat.
When the mixture is ready, put it in a cake tin.
Mix all the ingredients in a bowl.
When it is cooked take it out of the oven.

To talk about

Sometimes smells warn of danger. Think about such smells and say what you would do if you smelled them.

Alphabetical order

Put these words into alphabetical order. Remember: when two words begin with the same letter then we must look at the second letter.

c a ke   c o ok

1 King   knife   kettle
2 butter   bowl   beat
3 surprise   smell   sausage
4 oven   orange   old

5 thin   time   tea   tray
6 fat   flour   feast   food
7 lovely   lightest   laugh   legs
8 hot   happy   hungry   his

Opposites

Copy the sentences and choose a word to fill each space.

thin   sweet   small   cold   morning

1 The King is fat, but the cook is _____.
2 The soup is hot, but the ice cream is _____.
3 Sugar is _____, but vinegar is sour.
4 We have breakfast in the _____, but supper in the evening.

Copy and complete these opposites wheels.

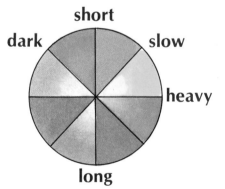

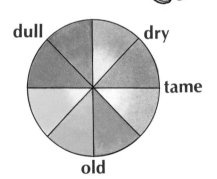

Writing

Copy this story filling in the missing words.

Once upon a _____ a thin cook made a cake for a fat _____. The cook mixed the cake, put the mixture in _____ tin and put it in the oven. Soon the _____ began to smell strange. The King ran into the _____. He found the cook crying. Something had gone wrong _____ the cake.

What do you think has gone wrong with the cake? Write a story about it.

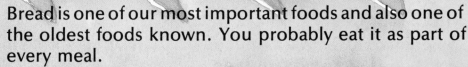

Bread is one of our most important foods and also one of the oldest foods known. You probably eat it as part of every meal.

Think of all the dozens of kinds of loaves there are to choose from. White loaves include farmhouse, cottage, tin, bloomer, barrel, French stick, cob, plait, Danish or Coburg. There are brown and wholemeal breads, milk, fruit, malt, cheese and soda breads. There are rolls, baps, buns, croissants and muffins. Can you think of any others?

UNIT 20

1 What are the main ingredients of most kinds of bread?
2 What is flour usually made from?
3 What other things can it be made from?
4 What sort of white loaves are mentioned in the passage?
5 Use a dictionary to find out what these words mean:
wholemeal malt croissants maize

Snacks This is a block graph of favourite snacks.
Look at it carefully and then answer the questions.

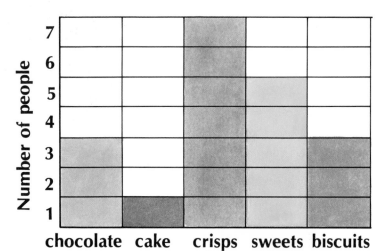

Number of people
7 6 5 4 3 2 1
chocolate cake crisps sweets biscuits

1 How many different types of snack are on the graph?
2 Which type of snack is the most popular?
3 How many like chocolate?
4 Which type of snack is the least favourite?
5 How many have been asked about their favourite food?
6 How many more people prefer crisps to biscuits?

Writing

What is your favourite food or meal? Find out where it comes from. Write about it.
Choose a day's menu for yourself. What would you like for each meal?
Add your writing to a class book called *Favourite Foods*.

Whatever its shape, size and colour, the basic ingredients of bread are the same. Flour, yeast, salt, fat and water are mixed together to form a dough, which is then shaped and baked.

Most bakers use flour made from wheat grain, which is ground into a fine powder. In some parts of the world, people also grind the grain of rye, maize or sorghum to make flour.

(From *Making Bread* by Ruth Thomson and Chris Fairclough)

An index

This is an index from a book about vegetables.
Note that the titles are in alphabetical order.

Vegetables	
Index	*page*
bean sprouts	30
cabbages	2
carrots	27
onions	6
peas	7
potatoes	24
spinach	10
sprouts	15
sweetcorn	11
yams	8

On which page would you learn about?

1 onions
2 yams
3 peas
4 cabbages
5 spinach
6 sprouts
7 carrots
8 bean sprouts
9 potatoes
10 sweetcorn

1.20a

Recipe for shortbread

Copy this recipe in your best handwriting. You can then make the shortbread at home or, if your teacher allows you, at school.

100g butter   100g plain flour   50g caster sugar

1 Heat oven to 170°C/325°F or Gas 3, and lightly grease a baking sheet.
2 Beat butter in a bowl until soft and then mix in the sugar.
3 Add sifted flour and work into a dough.
4 Roll dough into a circle approximately 1cm thick.
5 Place on a baking sheet and prick all over with a fork.
6 Bake for 45 minutes until lightly coloured.
7 Cut into slices, and allow to cool. Store in an airtight container.

DANGER!

Road signs tell drivers what to expect and what to do, without using words. Write down what you think all these signs mean.

Finding out

You can find all these signs and more in the *Highway Code*.

What do you think?

Read the following and use the information given to make a guess. You may already have done this when looking at the road signs above.

BEFORE I COULD STOP THE TRAFFIC A SILLY BOY RAN ACROSS THE ROAD IN FRONT OF A BUS. FORTUNATELY THE DRIVER STOPPED IN TIME. 1

IT WAS SO FOGGY I COULDN'T SEE THE LIGHTS OF THE CAR IN FRONT. 2

THE POSTMAN WAS VERY ANGRY. HE SAYS I SHOULD HAVE A SIGN ON THE GATE: BEWARE OF THE DOG! 3

WE HAD A SWIM AND THEN WE WALKED AS FAR AS THE LIGHTHOUSE. 4

1   Do you think she is   **a)** a lollipop lady?   **b)** a shopkeeper?
2   Do you think he is   **a)** a pedestrian?   **b)** a driver?
3   Do you think he is   **a)** a policeman?   **b)** a dog owner?   **c)** a postman?
4   Do you think they were   **a)** on a farm?   **b)** by the canal?   **c)** at the seaside?

Look carefully at the picture. Write a list in your book of all the dangers you find, and say what you think should be done to make the kitchen safe.

Missing words

Copy this passage and fill in the missing words.

Danger on the roads

Many children are killed in ＿＿＿＿＿ accidents each year. Many accidents are caused ＿＿＿＿＿ drivers going too fast, but many others are caused by ＿＿＿＿＿ being careless. You should never play near a road, and when ＿＿＿＿＿ want to cross you should always use the Green ＿＿＿＿＿ Code:

> 1   Find a safe place to cross.
> 2   Stand on ＿＿＿＿＿ pavement near the kerb.
> 3   Look all round for traffic ＿＿＿＿＿ listen.
> 4   If traffic is coming then let it pass. ＿＿＿＿＿ again.
> 5   If there is no traffic walk straight ＿＿＿＿＿ the road,
>   but keep looking and listening whilst you cross.

To talk about

Discuss safety in your school. What rules are there to help prevent accidents? Can you think of some new rules? What do you do when the fire alarm rings?

Writing

1   Illustrate your fire drill as a picture strip. Write a sentence or two for each picture.
2   Write and illustrate a *Safety at School* booklet for children in other classes to read. Warn them of as many dangers as you can.

Daddy Fell into the Pond

Everyone grumbled. The sky was grey.
We had nothing to do and nothing to say.
We were nearing the end of a dismal day.
And there seemed to be nothing beyond,
   Then
      Daddy fell into the pond!

And everyone's face grew merry and bright,
And Timothy danced for sheer delight.
'Give me the camera, quick, oh quick!
He's crawling out of the duckweed!' Click!

Then the gardener suddenly slapped his knee,
And doubled up, shaking silently,
And the ducks all quacked as if they were daft.
And it sounded as if the old drake laughed.
Oh, there wasn't a thing that didn't respond
   When
      Daddy fell into the pond!

Alfred Noyes

1 How did the family feel at the beginning of the poem?
2 Why did they suddenly begin to laugh?
3 Who else found Daddy's accident funny?
4 Do you think the drake really laughed? Why?
5 Do you think Daddy found it amusing? How do you think he felt?

To talk about

1 Has anyone ever laughed at something that happened to you?
   How did you feel?
2 Tell about something that made you laugh.
   Why did you find it so funny?

To do

Draw or paint an amusing picture of something you found funny.

Howlers

Look at these sentences. There is something wrong with them. Write them correctly.

1 John had a stake sandwich for his lunch.

2 We bought a table from a lady with carved legs.

3 Bobby's ant wears a green hat.
4 We went for a sale on the lake.
5 We saw a swarm of cattle at the farm.
6 Jane's hare was curly.

7 Mix the butter and flower together to form a dough.

8 We found a box belonging to a man made of wood.

Joining sentences

Use **and** or **but** to join these sentences.

1 Daddy fell into the pond. We all laughed.
2 He painted the ceiling very carefully. Some paint still dripped on him.
3 The clown did some funny tricks. He made us laugh.
4 We waited at the station for Aunty Margaret. She did not come.
5 We took an umbrella. It did not rain.
6 Daddy took us into the country. We had a picnic.
7 We looked everywhere for John's pen. We could not find it.
8 I went to bed early. I could not get to sleep.
9 I went to the shops. I bought two loaves of bread.
10 Sarah ran in the race. She won.

Writing

1 Look at this funny story. What do you think happened next? Tell the story in your own words. Here are some words to help you:

gardener   hose pipe   nozzle   jet   soaked.

2 Think of something funny that has happened to you, or to somebody else. Write about it. Make it so funny that your friends will laugh when they read it.

47

The Leader
Roger McGough

I wanna be the leader
I wanna be the leader
Can I be the leader?

Yipee, I'm the leader
I'm the leader

Can I? Can I?
Promise? Promise?

OK what shall we do?

1 What is amusing about the leader in this poem?
2 Do you know any leaders like this? Write about one.
3 If you were the leader of this gang what would you do?
4 Write a story about the adventures of a children's gang.

Chalky White

1 Write what you think Chalky is saying to himself in each picture.
2 Write the story of Chalky White and his binoculars, giving it an amusing ending.

Silly Billy

The pictures about Silly Billy are in the wrong order.
Write a sentence for each picture telling the story in the order it happened.

Joke Corner

Boy: Why are you wearing that silly hat?
Girl: It keeps the crocodiles away.
Boy: But there aren't any crocodiles round here.
Girl: Then it works, doesn't it?

Write out your favourite joke in your best handwriting.

Riddle-Me-Ree

Riddle-me! Riddle-me! What is that:
Over your head and under your hat?

1 When you have written the answer to this traditional American riddle, look at the foot of the next page to see if you were right.
2 Write your favourite riddle in your best handwriting.

Professor Kranky's Word Machine

Write the naming words the screen would show if the machine were:

- **a)** in the park
- **b)** in your classroom
- **c)** in your bedroom
- **d)** in the playground
- **e)** on a farm
- **f)** in a supermarket

If Professor Kranky changes the settings the machine could look at an object and give describing words for it. Write the describing words it would give for:

- **a)** your classroom door
- **b)** a dog
- **c)** yourself

Spot the Deliberate Mistakes

The picture has **ten** deliberate mistakes. Write a sentence for each one.

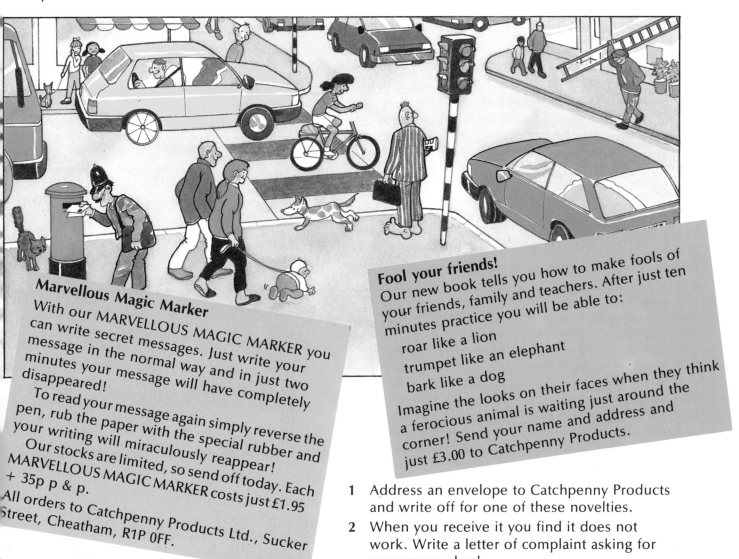

Marvellous Magic Marker

With our MARVELLOUS MAGIC MARKER you can write secret messages. Just write your message in the normal way and in just two minutes your message will have completely disappeared!

To read your message again simply reverse the pen, rub the paper with the special rubber and your writing will miraculously reappear!

Our stocks are limited, so send off today. Each MARVELLOUS MAGIC MARKER costs just £1.95 + 35p p & p.

All orders to Catchpenny Products Ltd., Sucker Street, Cheatham, R1P 0FF.

Fool your friends!

Our new book tells you how to make fools of your friends, family and teachers. After just ten minutes practice you will be able to:

- roar like a lion
- trumpet like an elephant
- bark like a dog

Imagine the looks on their faces when they think a ferocious animal is waiting just around the corner! Send your name and address and just £3.00 to Catchpenny Products.

1 Address an envelope to Catchpenny Products and write off for one of these novelties.

2 When you receive it you find it does not work. Write a letter of complaint asking for your money back.

Answer to riddle: Your hair

UNIT 24 The mice and the elephants

Long ago in India a herd of elephants found a deep, cool lake. They were delighted. They drank their fill and cooled themselves in its waters. The mice who lived by the lakeside were not so pleased. They were terrified of being crushed under the feet of the lumbering beasts. Something had to be done.

The oldest and wisest mouse decided to speak to the leader of the elephants. He climbed a high mound and called out. 'My lord the Moon is angry! You are trampling on his servants, the mice who guard his Moonlake.' He pointed to the water where the reflection of the moon trembled in the evening breeze. 'See the Great Lord Moon is angry. Kneel before him and beg his forgiveness!'

The leader of the elephants was greatly afraid. He knelt in the lake and bowed his head. The mouse smiled to himself and continued, 'Lord Moon, please forgive this ignorant creature.'

'Yes, please forgive me, Lord Moon,' wailed the elephant, 'We will leave your Moonlake immediately!' That very hour he led the herd far away, and the mice were never troubled again.

From an Indian folk tale.

1 Give two reasons why the elephants were delighted to find the lake.
2 Why do you think the mouse smiled to himself when he asked for the Lord Moon to forgive the elephant?
3 The pictures below are in the wrong order. Tell the story correctly by sorting the pictures and writing a sentence for each one.

To talk about

What do you think the mice said when the elephants arrived?
Pretend you are one of the mice and act out with your friends an emergency meeting of all the mice.

Animal's homes

What are the homes of these animals?
a) rabbit   **b)** horse   **c)** snail   **d)** lion   **e)** owl

Find out to which animals these homes belong:
a) burrow   **b)** sett   **c)** lodge   **d)** drey   **e)** eyrie

Saying things in a different way

Put a word in the empty space, so that the second sentence means the same as the first.

1   A mouse is not noisy.
    A mouse is _____ .
2   The elephants were in need of a drink.
    The elephants were _____ .
3   The mice were angry with the elephants.
    The elephants _____ the mice angry.
4   The mouse fooled the elephants.
    The mouse played a _____ on the elephants.
5   The elephants were gone in a short time.
    The elephants were _____ gone.
6   No one saw the elephants again.
    The elephants were _____ seen again.

Class names

Give each group a class name. The first two have been done for you.

1   elephant   mouse   cat   cow   *(animals)*
2   elephant   tiger   kangaroo   lion   *(wild animals)*
3   cow   pig   sheep   hen
4   cat   dog   gerbil   hamster
5   Labrador   Alsatian   Fox Terrier   Spaniel
6   Siamese   Persian   Burmese   Manx

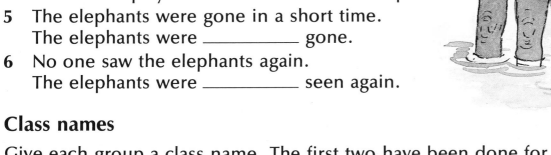

Writing

Moonlight

I saw moonlight lying on the ground,
I stooped and touched the ground with
my hand.
And found it was common earth,
Dust was in my palm.
P. J. Chaudhury   (India)

Suppose the moonlight changed the earth to magic dust. What powers might such dust have? Imagine you find this magic moondust. Tell the story of what happens.

PHOTOGRAPHS

1   What do you think is happening in this photograph?
2   Who do you think the man is?
3   Make a list of all the things that would be different if it were summer.
4   Describe in your own words what you can see in the photograph.

Test your memory
Study the picture carefully for a few minutes taking in as much detail as you can. Then turn to page 64 and answer the questions there without looking back at the picture.

1   Which of these is the picture mainly about?
    a)   a busy street
    b)   a man in danger
    c)   a broken clock
2   Write a story about how the man found himself in this dangerous situation and what happens next?

1   Give this picture a good title.
2   Describe a ride at the fairground, saying how you felt both during the ride and when you got off.

1 Which of these is the picture mainly about?
   a) a ship at the docks   **b)** using an old box   **c)** children playing cricket
2 Which things tell you that this is a very old photograph?

Test your memory
Study the picture carefully for a few minutes taking in as much detail as you can. Then turn to page 64 and answer the questions there without looking back at the picture.

To talk about
Suppose you were to travel back in time to this street. Choose three modern toys to take with you. Explain to the children how your toys work.

1 Give this picture a good title.
2 What does the girl look like in her make-up?
3 Why do you think she is wearing it?
4 Where might she be going, and what might she do?
5 How do you feel when you are in disguise?
6 Write a story about an adventure you have when in disguise.

A **plan** is a picture of an object as seen from above.
It is sometimes called a 'bird's eye view'.
What do you think these are plans of?

a)

b)

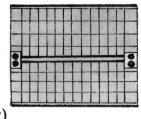
c)

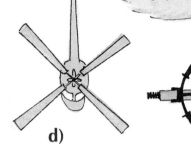
d)

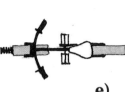
e)

Here is a plan of a classroom. There is also a **key** to help you understand it. Look at both of them carefully and then answer the questions in sentences.

Classroom plan

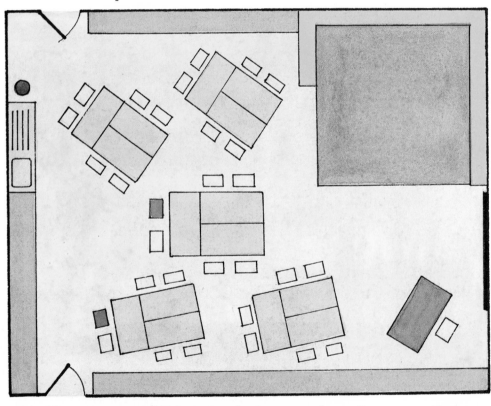

Key:
cupboards
sink
bin
carpet
bookshelf
desk
teacher's desk
chair
blackboard
door

1   How many children's chairs are there?
2   Is the sink next to the teacher's desk?
3   Is the teacher's desk near the door?
4   Does the classroom have a carpet? Where is it?
5   What is between the bin and the cupboard?
6   What is in front of the blackboard?
7   How many doors are there?
8   Are they opposite each other?

Draw a plan of *your* classroom.
Make a key to go with it.
Mark on the plan where you sit.

54

Word building

New words can be made by joining two words together.

> class + room = classroom
> cup + board = cupboard
> book + case = bookcase

Copy and complete these word webs to make new words. Use the word bank to help you.

thing   where   one   time   how   body   day

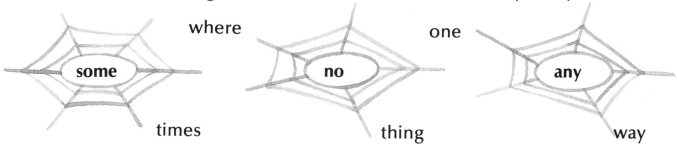

Choose **four** of the new words and put them in sentences like this:
  Has anyone seen my ruler?

Words with different meanings

Sometimes a word can have two different meanings.
  I am a **pupil** at Roundway School.
  The doctor shone a light into the man's **pupil**.
In the first sentence pupil means **a child who is taught at school.**
In the second sentence pupil means **part of the eye.**

Read these pairs of sentences and write the meaning of each word in heavy type. Use a dictionary to help you.

1a) I go to Roundway **School.**
  b) The sailors were pleased when they saw the **school** of dolphins.
2a) The old man was **mean** and cruel.
  b) Joseph did not **mean** to break the window.
3a) When I went into the house I switched on the **light.**
  b) The feather was so **light** it floated away.
4a) I got all my sums **right** today.
  b) Turn **right** at the traffic lights.

Writing

Look at the plan of the classroom again. Kay sits on the blue chair. Trace with your finger the way Kay would go to get to the blackboard. She would walk towards the far door, past the sink and round the tables to the blackboard. Write how Kay would get from her seat to these places in her classroom.
a) the bin   **b)** the carpet area   **c)** the teacher's desk   **d)** the red chair

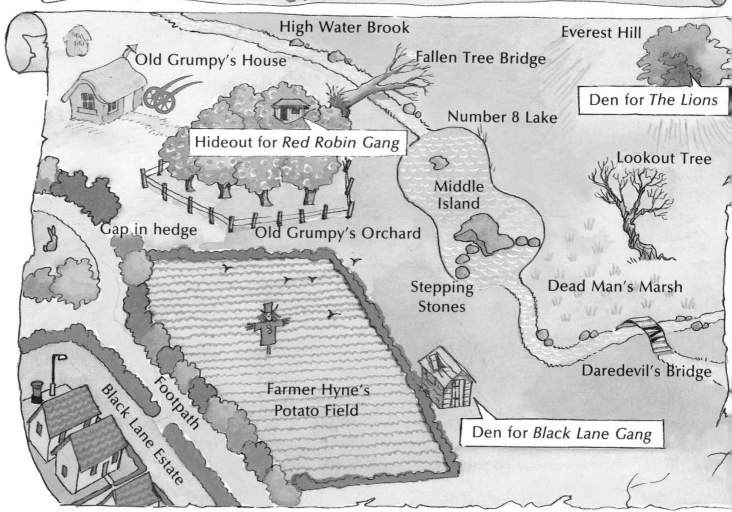

High Water Brook

Everest Hill

Old Grumpy's House

Fallen Tree Bridge

Den for *The Lions*

Number 8 Lake

Hideout for *Red Robin Gang*

Lookout Tree

Middle Island

Gap in hedge

Old Grumpy's Orchard

Stepping Stones

Dead Man's Marsh

Footpath

Daredevil's Bridge

Black Lane Estate

Farmer Hyne's Potato Field

Den for *Black Lane Gang*

This map shows the hide-outs of three groups of children: *The Lions, The Black Lane Gang* and *The Red Robin Gang.*

Look at the map very carefully and use it to help you answer the questions.

1 What have the *Black Lane Gang* used for their den?

2 What is grown in Farmer Hyne's field?

3 Which gang has a den on *Everest Hill*?

4 Why do you think the pond is called *Number 8 Lake*?

5 Where is the tree house?

6 What are the three ways of crossing over the water?

7 What do you think is grown in *Old Grumpy's Orchard*?

8 Which gang do you think might use the *Lookout Tree*? Say why you think so.

9 Describe how you would get from *Black Lane Estate* to the Red Robin's hideout.

10 Pretend you are a member of *The Lions*. Describe the way you would go to creep up on: **a)** The Black Lane Gang **b)** The Red Robin Gang.

To talk about

1 What name do you have for your gang or club?
2 What sort of den do you have? How is it built? What do you use for furniture?
3 Do you have secret passwords or codes? When and how do you use them?
4 Can anyone join your gang? Do you have a special 'initiation ceremony'?
5 Do you ever feel threatened by other gangs? Do you think gangs are a good or a bad thing? Why?

Directions chart

Look at this chart. It shows eight important places near to Black Lane School.
   Make a similar chart to this for your school. You will need a compass to find the eight directions.

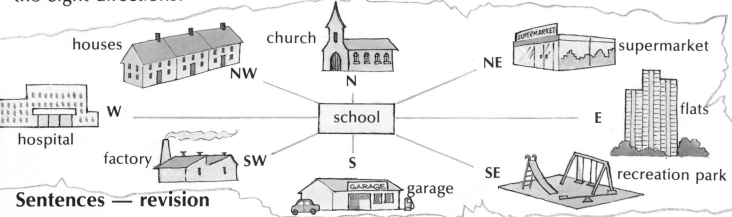

houses   church   NW   NE   supermarket
hospital   W   school   E   flats
factory   SW   S   SE   recreation park
garage

Sentences — revision

Copy these sentences correctly using capital letters, full stops and question marks where needed.

1 he is a member of the red robin gang
2 is the church north of the school
3 we live on wood street
4 let's follow the map to find our way to manchester
5 where do you live
6 no one knows i am the leader of the gang
7 mark and shofiq go to black lane school
8 the car went all the way north to scotland

1·28b

Writing

Look again at the adventure map. Pretend you are one of the gang leaders. Write an adventure story using the places on the map.

Things to do

Make an adventure map of your area. Use exciting names for all the places. Write about an adventure you have had there.

Sponsored Walk

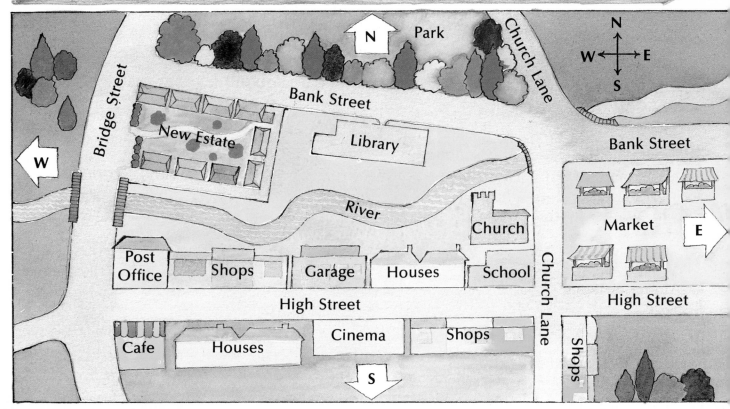

'I propose a sponsored walk,' said Debbie, 'to raise money for food.'

'For food?' echoed Howie.

'I'm not hungry,' said Steve.

'I am,' said Bet, who was listening outside the door.

Debbie groaned. 'It's not for us,' she said. 'It's for a special anniversary dinner. My Mum and Dad will have been married for fifteen years next Sunday and I propose we cook them a special meal with wine.'

They thought it over for a moment or two.

'Can we cook?' said Steve.

'Of course we can,' said Debbie. 'Everything comes frozen and all you do is put it into hot water and boil it.'

'Not ice cream,' said Howie. 'You don't boil ice cream.'

'I'll boil you if you keep being silly,' said Debbie.

Steve admitted that he liked the idea. 'Because the Gang will be doing two new things,' he said. 'The sponsored walk *and* the cooking. I'll write it down.'

He did so and Debbie was very pleased.

They discussed the walk and it was finally agreed that they would walk right round the village as many times as they could. Steve drew a map of the route and held it up for their approval.

'We start at the Post Office,' he said, 'go along the High Street as far as the school, turn left past the church, across the river and along by the library and back through the new estate. Is that agreed?' It was.

(From *More About the Gumby Gang* by Pamela Oldfield)

About the passage

Read these sentences about the passage. Are they true, false or doesn't the story tell you? Write **True, False** or **Does not say** for your answers.

1 Debbie was the one who suggested the walk.
2 Their parents had been married for nearly fifteen years.
3 Debbie was the oldest of the Gumby gang.
4 The money was for hungry people in Africa.
5 The walk was to finish at the Post Office.
6 The library is on High Street.
7 The children were going to cook beef for the special meal.
8 The children were going to walk around the village as often as they could.
9 Howie said, 'Everything comes frozen.'
10 The walk was to take place on Tuesday.

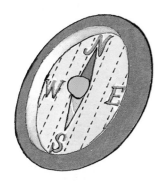

Look at the map and the compass points to answer these questions.

1 On which streets can you find: **a)** the library **b)** the cinema **c)** the church?
2 Name two buildings on the north side of High Street.
3 What can be found on the east side of Church Lane?
4 Which building is east of the new estate?
5 Which building is south of the church?
6 Is the new estate north or south of the river?
7 Is the market north or south of Bank St.?
8 Name three buildings that are east of the Post Office.
9 Which building is directly north of the cafe?
10 In which direction do I go if I start at the Post Office and want to go to:
   a) the new estate   **b)** the cafe   **c)** the school?

Writing

Imagine you lived next to the garage on High Street. Give full directions on how you would get to the park. Begin like this:

> I would go along High Street and turn left at the school.

Now give directions from the same house to: **a)** the market **b)** the new estate.
Trace on the map with your finger the route taken in the sponsored walk.
Suppose the Gumby Gang's sponsored walk were to take place in reverse, going up Bridge street from the Post Office. Write directions for this new route.

To talk about

Describe your daily route to school. Which streets do you use?
Describe how you would go from your house to the library, the park and or a friend's house.

From Caterpillar to Butterfly

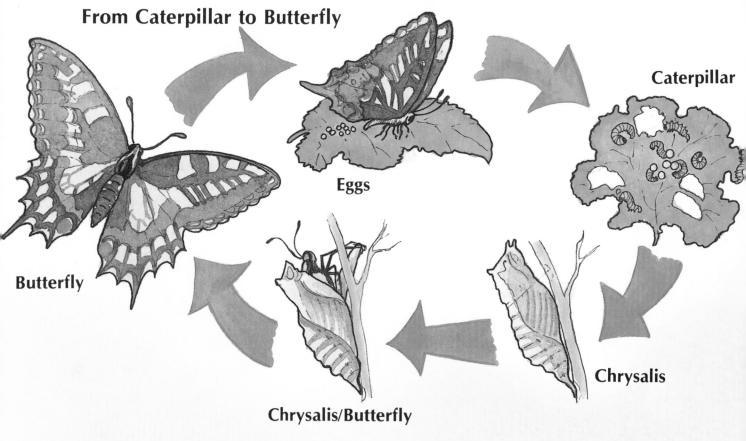

Eggs

Caterpillar

Butterfly

Chrysalis

Chrysalis/Butterfly

Use this diagram to help you finish these sentences. Copy the sentences into your book.

The adult butterfly finds a leaf on which to lay her _____ . Little _____ come out of the eggs.

The caterpillar eats _____ until it grows bigger. Then the caterpillar changes into a _____ . After about two weeks the _____ of the chrysalis splits and a _____ comes out. The butterfly lets its _____ dry in the sun. Then it flies away.

Using your dictionary

Here are some words all about insects. Use a dictionary to find out their exact meaning.

sting	antennae	larva	hornet
web	swarm	hive	cocoon

Now put these words into alphabetical order. Remember — if two words begin with the same letter then you must look at the second letter.

To talk about

Read this poem.

Tickle Rhyme

"Who's that tickling my back?'
said the wall.
'Me,' said a small
Caterpillar. 'I'm learning
to crawl.'
Ian Serraillier

1 Imagine you were the caterpillar on the wall. What dangers might face you?
2 Describe in your own words the life-cycle of a butterfly.
3 Are you afraid of any insects or mini-beasts? What is about them that frightens you? Do you think they might also be afraid of you?
4 Describe what you saw and how you felt when seeing a large spider.
5 Now imagine you are the spider. Describe what it felt when it saw you.

One and More than One

We say | one caterpillar, two caterpillars
but | one butterfly, two butterfl**ies.**

When a naming word ends in **-y,** we make it more than one by leaving off the **-y** and add **-ies.**

Make these into more than one.
1 One lady, two _____ .
2 One library, three _____ .
3 One party, two _____ .
4 One penny, several _____ .
5 One puppy, two _____ .
6 One family, four _____ .
7 One pony, three _____ .
8 One baby, two _____ .

Things to do

Choose from your library two books about insects and minibeasts. Find two types that have: **a)** wings   **b)** no legs.
Draw them in your book and write their names.

Writing

Imagine you have shrunk to only two centimetres in height. Use your ruler to check how really small that is! Now imagine you are lost in a garden and in great danger from all the minibeasts that live there. Write the story of your adventures.

The sun was up now and shining fiery-hot over the great yellow wasteland with its blue rocks and dead trees.

'Is you seeing them?' the BFG asked.

Sophie, squinting through the glare of the sun, saw several tremendous tall figures moving among the rocks about five hundred yards away. Three or four others were sitting quite motionless on the rocks themselves.

'This is Giant Country,' the BFG said. 'Those is all giants every one.'

It was a brain-boggling sight. The giants were all naked except for a sort of short skirt around their waists, and their skins were burnt brown by the sun. But it was the sheer size of each one of them that boggled Sophie's brain most of all. They were simply colossal. Far taller and wider than the Big Friendly Giant upon whose hand she was now sitting. And oh how ugly they were! Many of them had large bellies. All of them had long arms and big feet. They were too far away for their faces to be seen clearly, and perhaps that was a good thing.

'What on earth are they doing?' Sophie asked.

'Nothing,' said the BFG. 'They is just moocheling and footcheling around and waiting for the night to come. Then they will all be galloping off to places where *people* is living to find their suppers.'

'You mean to Turkey,' Sophie said.

'Bonecrunching Giant will be galloping to Turkey, of course,' said the BFG. 'But the others will be whiffling off to all sorts of flungaway places like Wellington for the booty flavour and Panama for the hatty taste. Every giant is having his own favourite hunting ground.'

(From *The BFG* by Roald Dahl)

1 Describe Giant Country in your own words.
2 What was it about the giants that Sophie found brain-boggling?
3 What do you think 'moocheling and footcheling' means?
4 The BFG does not use correct English. Choose three sentences with mistakes in them and write them correctly.
5 Describe what you think the 'Bonecrunching Giant' looks like.

To talk about

Why do you think giants go to Wellington for the 'booty' flavour, or Panama for the 'hatty' taste? Use your atlas to find these places.

Writing

Suppose one day you drank from a bottle labelled 'Giant Juice'. Describe what happened to you and the adventures you had.

Adding -ing

Look at the word 'moving' in the passage (line 5). If you want to add **-ing** to a word you must look at the last letter of the word.

In most cases we simply add **-ing**: throw — throwing   catch — catching

However, if the word ends in **e** then the **e** is left out when adding **-ing**: move — moving   shine — shining

Add **-ing** to each of these words:

| stare | walk | come | have | love | need | talk | shout | skate |

Now use each of the new words in a sentence.

Abbreviations

In the story the Big Friendly Giant is called the BFG for short. This is an abbreviation. Use a dictionary to help you find what these abbreviations stand for.

| 1 | SOS | 2 | cm | 3 | PO | 4 | TV | 5 | kg |
| 6 | RAF | 7 | USA | 8 | St | 9 | SE | 10 | USSR |

Initials

We can shorten our names by using special abbreviations called initials.

J ames **C** ourtney's initials are J.C.

L ouise **A** nn **W** ade's initials are L.A.W.

Write: **a)** your initials **b)** the initials of 3 of your friends.

Write the initials for these names:

| **a)** Mandy Livingstone | **b)** Jason Paul Davies | **c)** Su Lee |
| **d)** Caroline Mitchell | **e)** Michael Alan Clark | **f)** Sujat Khan |

Words with similar meanings

The story is about giants and many different describing words are used to show how big they are.
Here are some. Can you find them in the story?

| **tremendous** | **colossal** | **taller** | **wider** | **long** |

Make a list of all the words you can think of which describe how *large* things are.

Make a list of words which describe how *small* things are. Here are three to start you off: **small   tiny   little**.

Giants' Gallery

Make a Giants' Gallery in your classroom with pictures and information about famous giants such as Cyclops and Goliath.

Test your memory

Look carefully at the photographs in Unit 25 and then answer these questions.

Photograph 1 — Walking in the Snow (page 52)

1 How many people are there in the picture?
2 What is the man carrying?
3 Is there a car coming down the street?
4 Is the sun shining?

Photograph 4 — Street Cricket (page 53)

1 How many children are playing cricket?
2 How many girls are playing?
3 What is parked near the end of the street?
4 What kind of road surface is it?
5 Apart from the ship, what can be seen over the fence?

Revision word search

Copy this word search, putting in all the letters.
Hidden in the puzzle are twelve words. As you find each word draw a
ring round it. The clues will help you. The first one has been done for you.

1 The BFG is one.
2 A spider's home.
3 More than one lady.
4 Opposite to north.
5 Book + case
6 There are lots of these at Spooky Towers.
7 The opposite of heavy.
8 Not noisy.
9 A duckling's daddy.
10 The sound a bee makes.
11 St. Bernards, Alsatians, Labradors and Cocker Spaniels are all _____.
12 Put these words in alphabetical order:

   clock, cricket, custard, cork.

   Now look for the *third* word.

b	q	m	h	q	l	f	c
s	o	u	t	h	i	r	r
p	m	v	i	w	g	j	i
o	g	c	d	e	h	n	c
o	t	o	r	b	t	l	k
k	g	d	d	r	a	k	e
s	e	h	g	i	a	n	t
b	o	o	k	c	a	s	e